TAXI!

TAXI!

Simon Garner
Giles Stokoe

FRANCES LINCOLN

Frances Lincoln Limited
4 Torriano Mews
Torriano Avenue
London NW5 2RZ

TAXI!

British Library Cataloguing-in-Publication data

A catalogue record for this book is available from the British Library

ISBN 0 7112 1544 8

Printed in Hong Kong

9 8 7 6 5 4 3 2 1

contents

introduction

What is the best way to see London? From the top of a bus, from a helium balloon, from a stretched limousine or a giant Ferris-wheel? I think a good case can be made that the best way to see London is from the back of a licensed London taxi. London, after all, is a ground-level city. It isn't Manhattan, you don't need to crane your neck to get a sense of it. It exists in its details: in its winding alleys, street corners and hidden monuments. And a taxi is the perfect way of navigating this urban space. For a start you have an experienced pilot in front of you; a driver who knows every twist in the route like the back of his hand. Then there is the vehicle; a piece of history in itself, a rumbling, four-wheeled, diesel chariot that can turn on a sixpence and nudge its way through the narrowest of spaces. And inside this vehicle? There you have something quite unique: a small slice of privacy right in the middle of the busy streets, a rolling refuge from which to watch the city pass by. An impossibility? Not if you hail a cab.

However, what the passenger sees is only a very small part of a much bigger story. The licensed taxi trade is a massive undertaking which provides employment for a vast section of London's population. At the front line, of course, there are the 23,000 drivers and the 20,000 cabs that ply their trade on London's streets every day. But behind the drivers and the vehicles there stands a huge army of other people, all of whom, in their own way, are essential to the taxi trade. There are the officials responsible for regulating the trade, examiners, inspectors, students, the teachers at Knowledge schools, the car washers, the mechanics who keep the vehicles up to the required standard, the people who man the phone lines on the radio circuits and the café proprietors who are always on hand with a cup of tea and a bacon buttie. It is the aim of this book to reveal something of this often unacknowledged world. But before we get to that, a little history is in order.

TAXI!

The story of the London cab starts in the seventeenth century with the hackney coach. These coaches generally operated out of tavern yards but in 1633 a Captain Bailey made a significant breakthrough by bringing his four coaches out onto the street and setting up the first taxi rank in the Strand, outside the Maypole Inn. This launched the coachmen straight into their first industrial dispute. The Thames watermen were then the established form of transport in a city dominated by the river and the coachmen were cutting into their trade. London, however, was beginning to expand away from the river and the hackney coachmen were there to stay. In 1654 Oliver Cromwell set up the Fellowship of Master Hackney Coachmen by Act of Parliament and the cabbies' profession – at least, as far as statute goes – was born. Cromwell's Act remained in force for only three years but it was followed, in 1662, by a second Act under Charles II which required coaches to be licensed and restricted their number to 400.

Since then – barring the odd hiccup between Parliaments – the licensing of hackney coaches has continued to the present day, making the licensed taxi trade the oldest regulated public transport system in the world.

These original hackney coachmen, however, are not merely the fore-runners of the present day cabbies. In the latter half of the seventeenth century it was hackney coachmen who set up the original stage coaches (so called because they operated in stages, stopping at intervals to change the horses), connecting cities and towns in England. And it was out of the stages close to London that the London bus service developed. In fact, up to 1984 the Public Carriage Office, which regulates the licensed taxi trade, was also responsible for licensing bus drivers and conductors.

Hackney coaches continued in use until the early nineteenth century, when they were superseded by smaller, lighter cabriolets from France. The 'cab' had finally acquired its name (it wasn't to be called a taxi until taximeters were introduced in the early twentieth century). In 1831 the first London Hackney Carriage Act was passed and control of the trade was placed with the Metropolitan Police, where it remained for 169 years. With the advent of the Greater London Authority, however, responsibility will be transferred to 'Transport for London'.

At the same time as the first London Hackney Carriage Act was brought in, Joseph Hansom was working on the design of his famous Safety Cab, which he patented in 1834. It was variations upon this vehicle, and the four-wheeled Clarence or 'Growler', that dominated the cab trade into the twentieth century when they were finally usurped by the motor cab. And from then on everything was mechanical.

The earliest motor cabs were made by a variety of manufacturers: Unic, Renault, Ford, Vauxhall, Adler, Mascot, Beardmore and Herald were just some of the makes that could be found for hire on London streets. But once Austin entered the market in the 1930s with the High Lot, based on the Heavy 12 saloon car, they slowly began to establish predominance. First there was the Low Loader (shown below and so called because of the lowered floor pan), then the Flash Lot (because of its 'modern' styling), then the FX3 and finally the FX4. It is the FX4 that still remains the most common cab in use in London, albeit in a greatly

modified form as the Fairway. The FX4 was in production from 1959 right up until 1997 when it was superseded by the new TX1, making it, along with the Mini, one of the longest lived of British car designs.

So there you go. That is a very brief history of one of London's largest and most long-standing professions. The irony is, of course, that the profession is all too often ignored. When transportation in the capital is considered in Parliament it is invariably the tube system and the buses that come in for scrutiny while the taxi trade is largely left to fend for itself. And when changes are made – such as the introduction of wheelchair accessibility – it is the drivers that  have to pay for such changes. So the next time a cabbie offers you some unwanted advice, cut him a little slack and just agree with him (it is easier in the long run): remember that he belongs to a noble profession and be thankful that he knows where he's going.

Gro

A design classic, a triumph of engineering or an anachronism, the London taxi is nothing if not distinctive. As quintessentially urban as its drivers, this amiable, bug-eyed vehicle looks so familiar on London's streets that it would be hard to imagine the city without it. The cab, however, is not the product of natural evolution but a creature of statute. There is a reason why it is the way it is; and that reason is the strict Conditions of Fitness laid down by the cab trade's regulatory body: the Public Carriage Office. These standards cannot be satisfied by any standard production vehicle. If they could be, the traditional London taxi would have become extinct long ago, undercut by cheaper conventional models supplied by the major car manufacturers. As it is, however, the purpose-built taxi remains the workhorse of the London cab trade. In fact, if anything, its influence is spreading as other cities, such as Liverpool and Newcastle, have discovered that there is much to be said for using a vehicle that is specifically designed for its purpose.

wlers

Among other things, the Conditions of Fitness require that the turning circle must be less than 8.535m/28ft and more than 7.62m/25ft so the cab can U-turn off a central rank; that the distance in the passenger compartment between the highest part of the floor and the roof must be at least 1.3m/4ft 3½ in so that City gents don't have to take off their bowlers; that the top of the tread for any entrance must be at the floor level of the passenger compartment and must not be more than 38cm/15in above ground level when the vehicle is unladen, for ease of getting in and out; and that every cab must be wheelchair accessible.

Currently there are only two approved cabs in production: the curvaceous new TX1 and the older, angular Metrocab; though for the time being the classic Fairway, forerunner of the TX1, remains the most popular cab on the streets. Both are made by specialist firms and, among drivers, both have their adherents and their detractors.

"Nobody wants to drive the Metrocab – it looks like a bleeding hearse."

" To me the TX1 looks like a Noddy car. I'll stick with the Fairway."

There is no point in looking for a dented, damaged or even dirty cab on the streets of London. (You won't be offered a discount – and anyway, you won't find one.) To ensure that all cabs comply with the Conditions of Fitness, every taxi in London is thoroughly checked once a year by the Passing Station at the Public Carriage Office before it is issued  with a new licence. The test is three times more stringent than a standard MOT test for private vehicles. There are also roving inspectors who patrol the streets, crawling around under cabs and measuring how far the sliding window in the partition between the driver and the passenger opens (the maximum width must not exceed 11.5cm/4$\frac{1}{2}$in). If a cab is found to fall below the required standard a 'stop notice' will be issued and the cab will not be allowed to ply for hire until the defect is rectified and the cab has been submitted to the Passing Station for retesting.

I f you want to find a dented taxi, head out to Three Colts Lane in Bethnal Green, East London, where, under the railway arches, a string of dedicated taxi repair shops works to keep London's cabs up to the high standards required by the Public Carriage Office.

"It is all about money. Like with aircraft, you don't make any money when a taxi is not working."

 Sometimes I cover it all up with page-three girls.

"We sponsor a racing bike, a rugby team, a football team – and the Carriage Office."

TAXI!
28

"Are the drivers fussy? Well, we've got one guy comes in here, he's got a Bentley leather interior worth £16,000 in the back. Now he's fussy."

Strangely enough, the one thing that a black cab does not have to be is black.

"You get tourists coming over here and they have been told that in London they should only ever use black cabs. So that is what they do, they use black cabs. They won't get into a coloured one or one with advertising on it."

ince 1990, advertising has been permitted not just on the fold-down seats inside the passenger compartment, but also on the exterior of cabs. You get three sorts of advertising: single-door advertising (just on the front doors – it must be the same on both sides); double-door advertising (on both front and rear doors); and livery (where the whole of the cab can be painted).

However, advertising is not permitted on the boot of a cab in case it obscures either the licence plate or the registration number. Wherever it is intended to go, all advertising must be submitted to the Public Carriage Office for approval.

" We won't allow anything risqué or suggestive.
We had a problem with the French
Connection FCUK campaign. "

"People come to us with all sorts of wonderful visionary ideas: videos in the backs of cabs, screens in the rear windows, leaflets and vending machines. I believe that in Liverpool they have condom machines in the backs of cabs – we won't allow that here."

Obviously, because of the strict Conditions of Fitness, there are no longer any vintage cabs actually plying for hire on the streets of London. However, a number of these historic vehicles do still exist, and can be privately hired for weddings, film work and other occasions. Mike Berry, an enthusiastic collector, has a selection of Rolls Royces and vintage cabs for hire at his garage in New Barnet.

"We get people coming down here looking for a Rolls Royce for their wedding; then they see the taxis and they want one of them."

TAXI!
37

"We have the meter running when we do a wedding. If we're really quick we can do a whole wedding for 7*s*. 6*d*."

Even though there are no genuine vintage cabs working on the streets of London, you can travel in the next best thing. The Asquith is a modern reproduction of a vintage cab styled on the old Austin High Lot. But if you manage to hail one on the street consider yourself lucky: out of the 20,000 or so cabs plying for hire in London there are only eleven licensed Asquiths, and no more are being produced.

From the perspective of environmental awareness, there is a certain irony in noting that the first ever motorized cab, the Bersey – which appeared on the smog-ridden streets of London in 1897 – was electric. In fact, any self-respecting eco-warrior would ask why such cabs died out. In the case of the Bersey, however, there were good reasons. The machine was a monster: modelled on a horse-drawn carriage, it weighed over 14cwt., had a top speed of about 10 mph and rapidly acquired a reputation for breaking down. It was nicknamed the ''umming bird' because of the noise made by the electric motor.

The term 'Growler', though strangely appropriate to the rumble of a diesel engine, actually has its origin before the advent of motorized cabs. The growl in question refers to the noise made by a four-wheeled, one-horse carriage on a cobbled street. The Growler, properly called the Clarence, was introduced in the early nineteenth century.

Where

Becoming a London taxi driver is no mean feat. Before the licensing authority will consider your application you must be at least twenty years and three months old (you cannot have a licence until you are twenty-one), of good character (you have not been convicted of any criminal or traffic offences) and both physically and mentally fit. Only if you can satisfy these requirements can you begin the next, and most onerous, stage: acquiring the Knowledge of London. The Knowledge – as it is colloquially known – requires you to have a detailed recall of the 25,000 streets within a six-mile radius of Charing Cross Station. But it is not just the streets that you have to learn; you must also know the location of all clubs, hotels, hospitals, railway stations, parks, theatres, restaurants, courts, colleges, government buildings, places of worship and other destinations a passenger might require, as well as an understanding of the major routes outside the central area. And once you have learned all that, you must pass a stringent driving test.

to, gov'nor?

The process of acquiring the Knowledge starts with the blue book. Hardly a riveting read – unless, of course, you want to become a cabby – the blue book contains a list of 400 routes or 'runs'. Each run has a start and finish point and the Knowledge boy or girl's task is to learn the most direct route between them, paying attention to one-way streets and prohibited turns and noting any points of interest on the way. Learning these runs, however, is no mere academic feat that can be achieved by studying an *A to Z* map of London in your bedroom. A successful candidate will need to acquire practical experience of both the streets themselves and the nature of the examination. To do this, the Knowledge student will need not only to have the memory of an elephant; they will also require a crash helmet, a moped, a 'call-over partner' and the assistance of one of London's Knowledge schools.

"It's like a recurring nightmare – you have to keep at it. Go out on the bike six or seven times a week. If you leave off for a week or two you lose it."

At Knowledge Point on Caledonian Road in North London, the students learn how to 'call' the runs they have practised on their mopeds. They recite every street from the start to the finish of the route. This is a process that must be practised painstakingly with a 'call-over partner', a fellow student who tests their partner on the runs they have learnt. The aim is to stick as close to 'the cotton' as possible, the straight line formed between the start and finish points when a piece of thread is stretched across the map.

Having passed a written examination, the prospective cabby must embark upon a series of fifteen-minute oral examinations known as 'appearances'. These take place in small, white-painted rooms off the 'corridor of fear' at the Public Carriage Office in Penton Street, a strange world of Formica and big ties. For most Knowledge boys and girls this is a nerve-racking experience. The examiner will ask the candidate to call a number of runs and then, dependent upon success, they will fix the date for the next appearance.

"Travellers' Club to Kensington Manor Hotel? Pall Mall to Emperor's Gate, sir. Leave on the left Pall Mall. Right St James's Street. Left Piccadilly. Comply Hyde Park Corner. Leave by Knightsbridge. Bear left Brompton Road. Bear right Thurlowe Place. Forward Cromwell Gardens. Forward Cromwell Road. Left and right Stanhope Gardens. Right Gloucester Road. Left Southwell Gardens. Left Grenville Place. Right Emperor's Gate. Set down on right."

"'Appearances', there is a lot in that word. What the examiners are looking at is how you appear. You have to look like Mr Average cabby. We tell our students to take out their earrings and cover up their tattoos."

"The examiners are very tough. They are mostly ex-police officers. In my day there was one called Hedges; we used to call him 'the killer with a smile'."

Among Knowledge boys and girls the examiners have a fearsome reputation, and even veteran cabbies remember them with apprehension.

> ""They test your temperament too, they insult you to see what reaction they get.""

As the candidate progresses, the intervals between appearances slowly decrease from eighty-six to fifty-six days, from fifty-six to twenty-eight and so on down to fourteen days, until finally the examiner will inform the candidate that he or she has completed the Knowledge of London. Even then, however, the learning process is not at an end, for once the Knowledge of central London has been completed the candidate must go out and do the suburbs. This involves a further sixty-six runs covering the major routes outside the central area. Only then – provided that he or she has been successful in the driving test – will the candidate be issued with a green all-London badge.

"Every day we publish the questions asked that morning at the PCO [Public Carriage Office]. The Knowledge students all run in to see if there is anything new. It is a cat and mouse game; the examiners are always trying to outwit the students and the students are always trying to outwit the examiners."

If the thought of the exam is too daunting, it is still possible to become a London cab driver by studying for a yellow suburban badge rather than the green all-London badge. A yellow-badge candidate chooses one of the sixteen suburban sectors surrounding the central area and learns this sector in detail, starting with a list of thirty runs (rather than the 400 that are in the blue book). However, a yellow-badge driver is not permitted to pick up fares within six miles of Charing Cross Station, nor at Heathrow Airport.

"Some people lose it in the examination – it's like stage fright – they're asked a question and they just go blank."

"People do fail on the driving test. We had one student; he said, 'I failed on the hill start.' I said, 'How can you fail on the hill start when you've got an automatic cab?'"

On average it takes a student about three years to complete the Knowledge of London – though there are some who manage to do it faster. A suburban badge takes six months to a year to acquire.

"There's a saying – 'The harder I work the luckier I get.'"

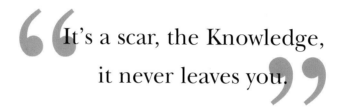

"It's a scar, the Knowledge, it never leaves you."

The Knowledge was first introduced in 1851 by Sir Richard Mayne, one of the two Police Commissioners appointed to oversee the hackney carriage trade, following complaints by visitors to the Great Exhibition that drivers did not know where they were going.

Strangely enough, before acquiring their badge, the one thing that a Knowledge student will not have done is to spend much time driving a cab; though he or she will have probably travelled something in the region of 20,000 miles on a moped. For many of the candidates the only experience they will have had of an actual taxi is when they take the driving test at the Public Carriage Office.

" New cabbies can be very nervous. Some drive around for days until they have the courage to pick someone up. They think they will get reported if they don't follow the cotton. "

It is sad but true, but women are very poorly represented in the taxi trade: out of the 23,000 drivers there are only about 250 women, that is about one per cent. But slowly the situation is changing: more and more women are doing the Knowledge.

"I've been a cab driver for eight years but I still get people saying, 'Oh, it's so nice to see a woman driver, that makes a change – is it your husband's cab?'"

Traditionally all new cabbies give the first job free. It is considered unlucky to keep your first fare. If the passenger insists on paying, the cabby will give the money to charity.

"Every cab driver remembers his first job; mine was Upper Street to Britannic Tower."

"Until you're sitting behind the wheel with a badge round your neck you don't know what it's like. It's a very strange feeling.

I sat there and looked down at my badge and I thought, 'I'm a London cabby!'"

Like any long-standing profession, over the years the taxi trade has built up its own vocabulary. The majority of drivers are Londoners after all, and you can't expect a Londoner to call a spade a spade if he or she can think of a better word to describe it. There are many expressions that are unknown to the general public and others which, though familiar, have obscure historical origins. Hackney, for a start, has nothing to do with the London borough of the same name but comes from the French word *haquenée*, meaning an 'ambling nag'. The word cab is short for cabriolet, the French word for a two-wheeled, one-horse carriage. And, in fact, there has always been a French connection: not only were the first two-wheeled carriages brought from France, but the first time that motor cabs were found in any numbers on the streets of London was in 1907 when the French-owned General Cab Company introduced a fleet of 500 Renault taxis. And cabs were never 'handsome' but 'Hansom', after Joseph Hansom who registered his Patent Safety Cab in 1834.

anguage

oranges and lemons *n.pl.* the major
arterial routes marked on the map in
orange and yellow

“ **If** a Knowledge boy is having trouble
calling a run you tell him to do it by
the oranges and lemons. ”

bilk *vb.* to defraud a driver of his or her fare. **~er** *n.* a person who seeks to defraud a driver of his or her fare

In 1832 a closed-in, two-wheeled cab was introduced onto the streets of London by Edward Boulnois. Unfortunately, the door of this cab was at the rear while the driver sat up front; passengers, therefore, found it easy to jump out before they had reached their destination. The cab became known as the 'bilker's cab'. It wasn't much of a success with drivers.

musher *n.* an owner-driver as opposed to a cabby who rents his cab

Today the majority of licensed cabbies are mushers. Of the 20,000 or so cabs on London's streets, only 6,000 are owned by fleets and rented out to drivers by the week or by the day. This situation, however, is a relatively recent phenomenon. Before the advent of affordable hire-purchase terms it was more normal for a driver to rent a cab from a proprietor. The relationship between proprietors and drivers was always a rocky one. In the late nineteenth and early twentieth centuries the amount charged to rent a cab was the source of a number of acrimonious strikes. However, in the 1930s, following a reduction in fares, an increase in petrol prices and police restrictions on the quality of vehicles, many cab proprietors went out of business. Today only a few fleets of a significant size remain.

butter boy *n*. a new cabby

"We call the new boys 'butter boys'. That's because they are taking the bread and butter from the older drivers. Or maybe it is because they've got the bread and they need the butter. I'm making this up you know. I should get it authenticated; I'm prone to tell lies – like all cab drivers."

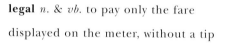

legal *n.* & *vb.* to pay only the fare displayed on the meter, without a tip

"It is still on the statute books that it is an offence to accept more than what is on the meter, but practically everybody tips these days. When somebody gives you just the metered fare you call it a 'legal' – 'He legaled me off.' And it doesn't make much difference to the Inland Revenue; they can  tell from the meter what your takings are, but whatever you declare they add ten per cent."

"The customers: well a 'him and her' is a couple, if it is just one person we call it a 'single pin' and a 'bowler hat' is a businessman."

"We've all got nicknames, nobody knows your real name: Paddy Two Thumbs, Norman the Foreman, The Beast, Night and Day, Basingstoke Bill, Northampton Terry, Video Jack, Silver Wizz."

broom off *vb.* to refuse to take a passenger

taxi *n.* [*Abbr.*] Taximeter cab

gasworks *n.pl.* the Houses of Parliament

wedding cake *n.* the Queen Victoria Monument in front of Buckingham Palace

face *n.* a slightly disreputable cabby specializing in airport runs and hotels

The word 'face' has its origins in the fact that before the advent of the feeder park, cabs were required to circulate around Heathrow Airport before they could pull onto the ranks at the terminals. However, they could only pull onto the rank when another cab left the rank. Certain cabbies would wait before they departed until they saw a face they recognized, thereby ensuring that their friends had work.

kipper season *n.* a period when trade is slack

" The kipper season is January, February and March when the game is very quiet. It's kipper season because we are so poor we can only have kippers for tea. Or perhaps it's because we are kipping rather than working. "

be on foul *vb.* to exceed the number
of cabs allowed on a rank

A sign at every cab rank states how
many cabs are permitted on that rank.
Drivers are required to move up as
vacancies occur and the drivers of the
first two cabs on the rank must stay
with their cabs and be available for
immediate hiring.

The Knowledge, too, has its own specialized vocabulary:

call-over partner *n.* a person with whom a Knowledge student can practise calling runs

cotton *n.* the most direct route between two points. **~ing up** *vb.* to practise runs with your call-over partner

run *n.* one of the 400 routes contained in the blue book that a cabby must learn to pass the Knowledge of London examination. **to call a ~** *vb.* to recite the route naming every street between the start and finish point

the drop *n.* the decrease in the length of intervals between appearances

point *n.* a place of interest that must be learnt to pass the Knowledge examination. Cabbies must know all the points within a quarter mile of the start and finish of each run

stopper *n.* a particularly difficult run

turn around *n.* a run involving reaching a destination on the right-hand side of a major road with prohibited right turns which requires the Knowledge student to know how and where they can turn around legally

wangle *n.* & *vb.* a scam perpetrated by garages whereby the garage lends a Knowledge student a cab for twenty-one days in order for the student to take the driving test on condition that the student rents a cab from the garage after he or she has obtained a licence

woosher *n.* someone who calls a run so fast that it is not possible to follow it

req *n.* [*Abbr.*] requisition

" It is what you are given when
you have finished the Knowledge of
London but you have still got the suburban
Knowledge to do. We call it the 'req' in
the trade – you're a complete wreck
when you've finished it. "

Reg

The history of the licensed cab trade is very much a story of a battle between a heavily-regulated profession and its unregulated competitors. In its early stages, it was the hackney carriage drivers who were muscling in on the trade of the Thames watermen, but today it is the unlicensed minicab that is threatening the licensed cabbies. For, while the licensed cabby is subject to a mass of statutory restrictions, the minicab trade is free to operate using whatever vehicles and drivers they wish. This situation, however, is set to change. Following the passing of the Private Hire Vehicles (London) Act 1998 by Parliament, minicabs in London are to be licensed. When the new regulations come into operation in the year 2000, all minicab drivers will have to wear an identity badge, be vetted for a criminal record, and pass a test showing they have general topographical skills. The vehicles will be tested, have to bear a license plate and operate through a designated control centre. What consequences this will have for the licensed trade only time will tell.

ulations

Although the 'for hire' or 'taxi' sign on a London taxi generally serves as a reliable indicator as to whether that cab is free, the light itself is not of any legal significance. When a moving cab is hailed, it is not legally obliged to stop whether the 'for hire' sign is illuminated or not because, as far as the law is concerned, a taxi is not plying for hire while in motion. Drunken punters therefore have no cause for complaint against a driver who fails to stop because he fears for his safety or upholstery. However, if the cabby responds to being hailed by stopping, he is then 'found standing in any street' and is under a duty to accept the fare

unless he or she is asked to drive more than six miles (or twenty if the journey begins at Heathrow Airport) or for longer than one hour. These regulations, stemming from the London Hackney Carriage Act of 1831, were not originally designed to benefit the passenger or driver, but the horse which would need to be fed and watered regularly.

TAXI!
96

NO PERSON WHO KNOWS HE IS SUFFERING FROM A NOTIFIABLE DISEASE SHALL ENTER A CAB WITHOUT PREVIOUSLY NOTIFYING THE OWNER OR DRIVER OF HIS CONDITION. NO PERSON HAVING THE CARE OF SUCH A PERSON SHALL PERMIT HIM TO BE CARRIED IN A CAB WITHOUT PREVIOUSLY INFORMING THE OWNER OR DRIVER. (PENALTY LEVEL 1.) IN ADDITION, THE COURT MAY ORDER COMPENSATION TO BE PAID TO THE OWNER OR DRIVER TO COVER ANY LOSS OR EXPENSE INCURRED IN THE DISINFECTION OF HIS VEHICLE... THE PHRASE 'NOTIFIABLE DISEASE' MEANS THE LIST FOLLOWING, OR ANY OTHER DISEASE MADE NOTIFIABLE BY THE SECRETARY OF STATE UNDER REGULATIONS TO BE MADE UNDER SECTION 13 OF THE PUBLIC HEALTH ACT OF 1984.

CHOLERA, PLAGUE, SMALLPOX, THYPHUS, RELAPSING FEVER, PARATYPHOID FEVER, TYPHOID FEVER, LASSA FEVER, SCARLET FEVER, YELLOW FEVER, VIRAL HAEMORRHAGIG FEVER, ACUTE ENCEPHALITIS, ACUTE MENINGITIS, ACUTE POLIOMYELITIS, ANTHRAX, DIPHTHERIA, DYSENTERY, LEPROSY, LEPTOSPIROSIS, INFECTIVE HEPATITIS, MALARIA, MARBURG DISEASE, MEASLES, ANY FOOD POISONING, TETANUS, TUBERCULOSIS, RABIES, OPTHALMIA NEONATORUM AND WHOOPING COUGH.

(Public Health [Control of Disease] Act 1984, s. 33)

THE FOLLOWING OFFENCES ARE PUNISHABLE BY PENALTY LEVEL 1 OR TWO MONTHS IMPRISONMENT:

A) WANTON OR FURIOUS DRIVING

B) CAUSING HURT OR DAMAGE TO ANY PERSON BY CARELESSNESS OR WILFUL MISBEHAVIOUR

C) DRUNKENNESS DURING EMPLOYMENT

D) USE OF INSULTING OR ABUSIVE LANGUAGE DURING EMPLOYMENT

E) USE OF INSULTING OR ABUSIVE GESTURES DURING EMPLOYMENT

F) ANY MISBEHAVIOUR DURING EMPLOYMENT

A JUSTICE MAY ORDER THE PROPRIETOR OR THE DRIVER OF THE CAB TO PAY A SUM NOT EXCEEDING £10 AS COMPENSATION FOR ANY 'HURT OR DAMAGE' AS IN (B) ABOVE. IF SUCH ORDER IS MADE AGAINST THE PROPRIETOR, HE MAY RECOVER THE AMOUNT PAID IN COMPENSATION FROM THE DRIVER.

(The London Hackney Carriage Act 1831, and The London Hackney Carriage Act 1843)

In sharp contrast to the unlicensed trade, the fares demanded by licensed cabbies for any journey within the Metropolitan Police District or the City of London have always been fixed by Parliament. The fare is calculated both by distance and time and extras are payable for additional passengers, items of luggage over 60cm/24in long and for hirings on evenings, nights, weekends and public holidays. For long journeys outside the Metropolitan Police District, the price is negotiated with the driver.

> **"Someone made an application suggesting that during the last World Cup the fares should be raised, because cabbies were being deprived of watching the football."**

This suggestion was not without historical precedent. In 1761 the hackney coachmen and Sedan chairmen of London applied to the Privy Council to be able to raise their fares during the coronation of George III. When the Privy Council refused the request, the coachmen and chairmen threatened to refuse to work. Eventually a face-saving compromise was reached, whereby the Privy Council did not put up the fares but a number of prominent citizens voluntarily undertook to pay extra to coachmen and chairmen who would work through the coronation.

"Back in the 1960s Harold Wilson wanted to nationalize the taxi trade. He was going to give drivers a liveried uniform and a salary. I said, 'Fine, do it quick, I can spend all my time in Regents Park with the dogs.'"

Hyde Park might be the largest open space in inner London, but for 230 years it was off-limits for cabbies (at least in the course of their employment). Following an incident in 1695 involving certain unruly ladies in a hackney coach – presumably the seventeenth-century equivalent of a hen-party – hackney coaches were banned from the park. They were only allowed in again in 1924.

Don't worry if you leave your wallet in the back of a licensed London taxi. As with everything in the trade, there are strict rules governing the treatment of lost property. In fact, a cabby is required by law to search his or her cab after each hiring. If the cab driver finds anything, it must be taken to a police station within twenty-four hours stating where and when the item was found. It will then be passed on to the Public Carriage Office where, for a small charge, it can be collected by the (rather unfortunately titled) 'loser'.

Last year the Lost Property section at the Public Carriage Office received 4000 mobile phones, 1000 wallets, 300 umbrellas and a Turkish hookah. Over half of the items found were successfully returned to their owners.

Should an item remain unclaimed for more than three months it will be offered to the cab driver, with the exception of any item capable of containing personal information (such as mobile phones or laptop computers) – these have to be destroyed.

"One of the strangest things was the candle rack from a church. It turned out that two teenage girls had stolen it and then jumped into the back of a cab. But when the cabby looked round and saw what they had with them, they ran off. It was just down the road from the Lost Property office and so he brought it straight in. We immediately rang up the nearest Catholic church down in Amwell Street and asked the priest if he was missing a candle rack. He said, 'Yes, I've just seen it going out the door.'"

"Sometimes people use cabbies just to get rid of things. We once had an old TV, two chairs and a table. Someone had hailed a cab and told him to take them round to a friend's house. The cabby couldn't find the friend's house so he took them

back, but when he got there the person who had hired him had vanished."

Cabbies are not required to wear seat-belts when they are at work. However, they must wear them when they are 'travelling to and from work'. Obviously there are certain niceties of definition here; but as a general rule it can be said that if you see a cabby with a seat-belt on, he or she is not for hire. All cabs are now fitted with seat-belts in the passenger compartment.

As well as inspecting taxis, examining the Knowledge and running the Lost Property Department, the Public Carriage Office is also the place to go if you have a complaint about a licensed cab driver. The Complaints Department receives 1,200 complaints a year. This is less than four a day which, considering the size of the profession, is pretty impressive. Most are for 'devious routes', 'taking more than the proper fare', 'refusals', 'misbehaviour' and 'abuse'. If a complaint is substantiated the cabby in question will be warned, and if he continues to offend his license can be suspended or revoked. And if a cabby loses his ordinary driving licence, his taxi licence will also be revoked.

"Unfortunately many of the complaints are about the same driver, while there are hundreds of drivers out there who have been driving for fifty years and have never had their card marked."

It is a popular urban myth that cabs are still required by law to carry a bale of hay. This might be an appealing anachronism, but sadly it has no basis in reality. The last horse-drawn hackney carriage surrendered its licence on 3 April 1947 and since then all London cabs have been powered by the internal combustion engine.

Victorian notions of privacy lasted for a long time in the London cab trade. It was not until 1959 that the first cabs appeared with internal rear-view mirrors and, even then, they were set low on the bulkhead to prevent the cabby seeing into the passenger compartment (and, consequently, much of the road behind). When rear-view mirrors became a legal requirement in 1968 many cabbies were so accustomed to driving without them that they turned them to the ceiling to avoid intruding on their passengers.

THE RESTORATION
OF THIS SHELTER
IN 1987 FOR THE
CABMEN'S SHELTER FUND
WAS PROMOTED BY THE
HERITAGE OF LONDON TRUST
WITH GENEROUS ASSISTANCE FROM
THE FORMER GREATER LONDON COUNCIL,
THE BEDFORD ESTATE,
THE SWAN TRUST,
MISS HAZEL WOOD
AND
BRENDA BANCROFT
AND HER FAMILY

PRESENTED BY
SIR SQUIRE BANCROFT
1901

Cabme

Dotted across London, and looking more like miniature cricket pavilions than cafés, the cabmen's shelters have been around for more than 100 years. Their history dates back to a snowy morning in January 1875 when, so the story goes, the editor of *The Globe Newspaper*, a Captain J. Armstrong, sent his manservant out to fetch a cab. Much to Captain Armstrong's frustration it took the manservant over an hour to return. Apparently, the cabbies, freezing while sitting on top of their Hansom Cabs, had abandoned their vehicles and sought refuge in a grog shop where they were warming themselves with tots of rum. When a sober driver was finally found to take Captain Armstrong to work he pondered this inconvenience and in a splendid example of double-edged Victorian benevolence decided to do something about it. With a group of colleagues he founded the London Cabmen's Shelter Fund. The first shelter was opened on 6 February 1875, located, not surprisingly in Acacia Road, St John's Wood, close to Captain Armstrong's home.

n's shelters

Between 1875 and 1950, some forty-seven shelters were erected in London funded by donations from a number of prominent citizens, including King Edward VII, the Earl of Aberdeen and a variety of Members of Parliament. There are only thirteen of the shelters left but they are still owned by the London Cabmen's Shelter Fund which is now part of the Transport and General Workers' Union. Nine of these have been restored by the Heritage of London Trust; most recently the shelter in Warwick Avenue, Maida Vale.

"Most of them were rotten underneath, they had to be lifted up and then a whole new floor was built under them. It was all done properly, it had to be English Oak not African hardwood or anything like that. The one in St John's Wood, that was built down in Mitcham and brought up on a low-loader."

"We got the Duke of Westminster to open one of them. We had all these posh folk hanging about. They loved it. They'd have a bacon buttie and say, 'I haven't had one of these since I was at Prep School.'"

Since they were open into the small hours of the morning, cabmen's shelters were often frequented by well-known personalities looking for a late night cocoa. The explorer, Sir Ernest Shackleton, was a regular visitor to the shelter at Hyde Park Corner. Before his last expedition, the cabmen presented him with a set of pipes and a pipe rack. Shackleton's letter of thanks hung on the wall of the shelter for many years, right up until the shelter was demolished to make way for the Hyde Park underpass in the 1960s.

“You get the same old crowd. They come in here and bore each other to death. They're all right so long as you laugh at their jokes.”

Under the roar of the Westway, just past the Westminster car pound and tucked up close to Royal Oak Station, you will find the modern equivalent of the cabmen's shelters. Here there is a miniature taxi city that caters for all a cabby's needs. There's plenty of parking, a car wash, mechanics, a dealership and, most important of all, the Cab-hut; a twenty-four hour canteen serving the drivers with round-the-clock sustenance. But don't try going there: it is members only and you won't be let in without a badge.

A person getting into a cab at Heathrow Airport probably doesn't ask where that cab came from. He or she will most likely be unaware that the driver might have been waiting for several hours before arriving at the rank. Nor will the customer know that the cab driver has already had to pay £2.15 for the privilege of being able to pick up a fare, or that his or her progress has been regulated by a hi-tech computer system since arriving at the airport. But that, in fact, is what will have happened. Out on the Northern Perimeter Road, between the A4 and the northern runway and tinged with the smell of burning rubber (from the planes not the cabs), is the feeder park; a twilight zone for cabbies where they wait for their number to come up on the screen that tells them which terminal to attend.

wo hours waiting time might seem excessive, but for many cabbies it is a welcome break, a chance to get out of the driving seat and stretch their legs, catch up on lost sleep, have a bite to eat, play cards or even study for an Open University degree. And at the end of it, who knows, that dream job might just come walking out of Terminal Three.

" The longest one I've ever heard
of was to Cornwall for £300. "

At the Cab-In, manned by traffic wardens from the Metropolitan Police, drivers buy tokens that permit them to pick up a fare at Heathrow. The tokens are sold in batches of ten. But if the cabby gets a local job and is back at Heathrow within one hour, he or she does not have to queue again at the feeder park but is allowed straight back onto the rank.

TAXI!
132

There are even stories – unsubstantiated, of course – of new cabbies going out to the feeder park and going home on the tube after losing their cab at cards.

METROCAB

"You'll never gu
who I had

Is there any such thing as a typical cabby? No, not really. Cabbies come from all walks of life and beneath the cockney charm (my favourite oxymoron) you will find that few of them correspond to the traditional stereotype. But then, how much can you really tell about someone when all you can see is the back of their head? Certainly, I've never had one who has refused to go south of the river. One thing is for sure though, the life of a working cabby is a strangely lonely existence. It isn't for everyone. There is a significant number of people who, having battled their way through the Knowledge, find the reality of sitting in a cab all day too much to bear. And so perhaps it is because of the isolation that cabbies, once they are given an opportunity to talk, are never short of an opinion or a story. (If there's a collective noun for a group of cabbies, it should probably be a grumble.) Mind you, if cabbies can be voluble on most matters there is one subject over which they are invariably tight-lipped: a cabby will never tell you how much he or she earns.

ess
in my cab!"

"The most famous customer I ever had was Marlon Brando, back when he was in his prime. I picked him up in Piccadilly. When he paid he just held out his hand with a big heap of coins and said, 'Help yourself.'"

“People change at night; it brings out the worst in them. But nights are easier because there's no traffic. You either put up with the traffic during the day or the drunks at night.”

"We're the only profession that is truly united – we all hate the public."

"I hate journalists – there are three people who make money out of other people's misery: undertakers, journalists and solicitors. And you can quote me on that."

"I picked up this man and his kid at Heathrow. They wanted to go into central London. He looked at the meter and saw it said £1.40. So I set off down the M4 and it was a cold day so I had my hand on the dashboard. And when we got into London he gets a policeman and says, 'That driver's got a magnet in his hand. Every time he taps his fingers the price goes up by twenty pence.'"

"I'd never done a job where you get tipped before. As far as I was concerned, the customers were the most generous people I'd ever met."

"I did have this woman once, she said, 'I've got no money, can I work it off?' It was a bit sad really, she was well past her sell-by date. I said, 'No love, have it on me.'"

"The new cabbies have it easy. Compared to the old cabs the cabs today are more like limos, what with air conditioning and everything. I used to drive an FX3. They were open at the front. In the winter they were freezing and in the summer they were boiling. And you had to tie the luggage on to the platform. I once lost a whole load of luggage going round the Aldwych; that was pretty embarrassing. It belonged to two American tourists. And the cabs were all manual then, there weren't any automatics. They had this really long gear stick that would vibrate like hell; you had to keep your arm away from it, it could break your wrist if you weren't careful."

"I guess you have probably noticed; but cab drivers tend to shout even when they haven't got their back to someone."

"I like City people. They know the score. They know what to pay and they don't complain."

"We don't have to take cheques. And the customer is supposed to have the correct change. If you give me a £50 note I'm entitled to take the money, ask for your address and send you the difference. When I tell the punters that they soon come up with the right money."

"I did have these five guys in the City. When they got out they all started arguing about who was going to pay. Then they started laughing and began to wander off. The last thing you can do is get out and run after them – but luckily I'd pulled up in front of a police van, so I told the policemen. They went after them, put them into the back of the van and brought them back. And I was still sitting there with the meter running."

TAXI!
151

"If you're single, this job is terrific. But if you've got a home to keep there is always someone saying, 'Ain't it about time you went to work?' I come out  with the hump every morning. Mondays is my worst day."

"When I die I want my ashes spread in Oxford Street. I've been up and down there so many times – I've spent half my life in Oxford Street."

" You used to get the hookers on Park Lane. They used to get in the back with a punter and say, 'Up the top and around.' And by the time you got back they'd have done the business.  They were generous too. When they paid they'd always say, 'Here, cabby, have a drink on me.' Mind you, that was years ago. You don't get any of that now. "

"Yes, we get quite a lot of celebrities. I used to carry a camera so I could take pictures. But then I thought, 'They're just normal people. They probably just want to be left alone.'"

" My first cab was an FX3; it had a mechanical meter, no indicators – they came later. There were a lot of hand signals then – I suppose there's still a lot of hand signals but they're not the same. . . "

"A book on cabbies? That's a bit like doing a book on wild animals in the zoo – only here they're not in cages."

Taxi organizations and

Where to find the Cabmen's Shelters

Albert Bridge, SW3
Grosvenor Gardens, SW1
Hanover Square, W1
Kensington Road, SW7
Kensington Park
   Road, W11
Northumberland
   Avenue, WC2
Pont Street, SW1
Russell Square, WC1
St George's Square, SW1
Temple Place, WC2
Thurloe Place, SW7
Warwick Avenue, W9
Wellington Place, NW8

Further Reading

The History of the London Cab Trade
by Philip Warren
(1995) Taxi Trade
Promotions Ltd
Price: £12.95

By mail order from:
Taxi Trade Promotions Ltd
431 Caledonian Road
London
N7 9BG
0207 700 5681

Complaints about a Licensed London Taxi

Public Carriage Office
15 Penton Street
London, N1 9PU
0207 230 1631

Radio Circuits

Dial-a-Cab
0207 253 5000

Computer Cab
0207 432 1432
(credit card bookings)
0207 432 1463
(account enquiries)

Radio Taxis
0207 272 0272

Vintage Taxis

Mike Berry's Classic Cars
0208 449 2954

Vintage Style Limousine
Taxis
0207 739 2850

London Vintage Taxi
Association
01438 722372

Property Lost in a Licensed London Taxi

Metropolitan Police Lost
Property Office

15 Penton Street
London, N1 9PU
0207 833 0996

Guided Tours in a Licensed London Taxi

Taxi Tours
0937 672835
web site: http://www.
taxitours.demon.co.uk

Taxi World Ltd
07957 460029

Black Taxi Tours
of London
0207 289 4371

Applications to do the Knowledge should be addressed to:

Public Carriage Office
15 Penton Street
London, N1 9PU
0207 230 1652

Knowledge Schools

Knowledge Point
431 Caledonian Road
London
N7 9BG
Principal: Malcolm
Linskey
0207 700 5682

Green Badge
42 Clapham Manor
  Street
London
SW4 6DZ
Principal: EA Eldon
0207 498 5885
0207 701 7078

Knowledge College
32 Penton Street
London
N1 9PU
Principal: John Godfrey
0207 698 8182
0973 313148

KPM UK Taxi School
114 Vallance Road
London
E1 5BL
Principal: Mrs Jan Sadler
0207 247 8940

Paddington Knowledge
  School
1 Kensal Road
London
W10 5EG
Principal: Mr Pegman
0208 968 0575

Point Man School
Supreme House
Stour Wharf
Stour Road
London
E3 2NT
Principal: John Godfrey
0208 550 0617
0973 313148

Taxi Drivers' Organisations

Licensed Taxi Drivers
Association
0207 286 1046

London Cab Drivers
Club
0207 278 4414

Transport and General
Workers Union
0207 387 7274

The Company of
Hackney Carriage
Drivers
0207 460 6665

Acknowledgments

Thanks to Philip Warren, whose *The History of the London Cab Trade* (1995, Taxi Trade Promotions Ltd) was an invaluable source of historical information; the Public Carriage Office; the Metropolitan Police Lost Property Office; Knowledge Point/Taxi Trade Promotions; Mike Berry's Classic Cars; The National Motor Museum at Beaulieu; the Heritage of London Trust; the London Cabmen's Shelter Fund; the traffic wardens at Heathrow Airport and to all the drivers who took the time to talk to us. Thanks also to Christopher Westhorp for his invaluable opinions.

Words, wit and wisdom

All quotations featured in this book were diligently compiled over Formica tables and instant coffee and come direct from the mouths of cabbies and other members of the licensed taxi trade. The voices belong to: Malcolm Linskey, Tony Norris, Wendy Wright and Derek O'Riley at Knowledge Point/Taxi Trade Promotions; Mike Pearl and Tony Bishop at the Public Carriage Office; Lynn Jones at the Metropolitan Police Lost Property Office; Mike Berry and Ralph at Mike Berry's Classic Cars; Peter Raymond from the London Cabmen's Shelter Fund; the traffic wardens at Heathrow Airport; Ruth at the Kensington Park Road Cabmen's Shelter (thanks for the tea); John at C&S Taxis Ltd; Bernie Joel at Nationwide Taxi Sales; Al Gunning at Taxi Tours; Alan Parker; Lawrence O'Toole; Monty Morris; Ron Wisker; Jackie 99; South African Bernie; Mickey Mouse (not his real name) and a number of other drivers, mechanics, Knowledge boys and girls who, for whatever reason, preferred to remain anonymous.